W9-AUU-514

Creative Days

Program Consultants

Stephanie Abraham Hirsh, Ph.D.
Associate Director
National Staff Development Council
Dallas, Texas

Louise Matteoni, Ph.D.
Professor of Education
Brooklyn College
City University of New York

Karen Tindel Wiggins
Social Studies Consultant
Richardson Independent School District
Richardson, Texas

Renee Levitt
Educational Consultant
Scarsdale, New York

STECK-VAUGHN
C O M P A N Y
A Subsidiary of National Education Corporation

MOMENTS IN AMERICAN HISTORY

Creative Days

BY
Melissa Stone

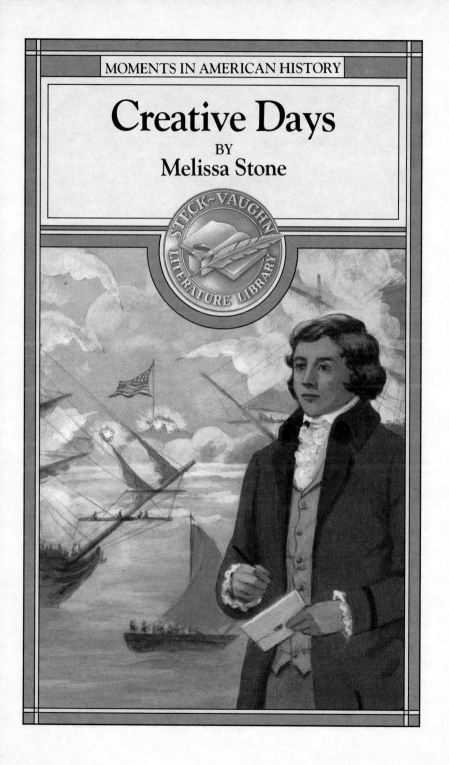

STECK-VAUGHN
LITERATURE LIBRARY

Steck-Vaughn Literature Library
Moments in American History

RISKING IT ALL
REBELLION'S SONG
CREATIVE DAYS
RACING TO THE WEST
YOU DON'T OWN ME!
CLOUDS OF WAR
A CRY FOR ACTION
LARGER THAN LIFE
FLYING HIGH
BRIGHTER TOMORROWS

Illustrations: Brian Pinkney: pp. 8-9, 11, 13, 15, 16-17, 19; Jim Pearson: pp. 20-21, 23, 24, 27, 28-29, 31; Christa Kieffer: cover art, 32-33, 34, 37, 39, 40, 43; D.J. Simison: pp. 44-45, 46, 49, 51, 53, 55; Steve Cieslawski: 56-57, 59, 60, 62, 65, 67; Rae Ecklund: pp. 68-69, 70, 73, 75, 76, 79.

Project Editor: Anne Souby

Design: Kirchoff/Wohlberg, Inc.

ISBN 0-8114-4077-X (pbk.)
ISBN 0-8114-2667-X (lib. bdg.)   LC 89-110887

Copyright © 1989 Steck-Vaughn Company.
All rights reserved. No part of the material protected by this copyright may be reproduced or utilized in any form or by any means, electronic or mechanical, including photocopying, recording, or by any information storage and retrieval system, without permission in writing from the copyright owner. Requests for permission to make copies of any part of the work should be mailed to: Copyright Permissions, Steck-Vaughn Company, P.O. Box 26015, Austin, Texas 78755.

Printed in the United States of America.

3 4 5 6 7 8 9 0 UN 98 97 96 95 94

CONTENTS

1800

◄ BENJAMIN BANNEKER
By day, he farmed. At night
he taught himself geometry
and astronomy.
(1730–1800)

FRANCIS SCOTT KEY ►
The blaze of battle moved
him to write a glorious
national anthem.
(1814)

◄ FREDERIC TUDOR
He knew he could make
money selling ice in the
tropics.
(1806–1833)

◄ **CHARLES GOODYEAR**
He discovered how to keep
rubber from changing with
the temperature.
(1834-1844)

SAMUEL F. B. MORSE ►
Instant communication
became a reality with
his telegraph.
(1830–1844)

◄ **ELIZABETH BLACKWELL**
She knew she could be a
good doctor. All she wanted
was a chance.
(1847–1857)

BENJAMIN BANNEKER

EARLY BLACK SCIENTIST

Could anything be more beautiful? That full moon and all those stars—like thousands of brilliant diamonds on black velvet. But it's peculiar. The sky at night doesn't always look the same. The autumn sky is different from the spring sky. The stars must move. How long does it take a star to move all the way across the sky? I wonder if I could figure out the pattern of movement. I bet if I watched the skies long enough, I could figure it out.

B ENJAMIN," warned his mother, "it's not safe for a black boy to be seen too far from home. You can't just walk into town. You never know when a slave trader might kidnap you and sell you as a slave."

Benjamin Banneker shuddered. He knew that he and his family were free blacks, but he also knew about slavery. Many of the blacks living in Baltimore County in the 1730's were slaves. Benjamin's own father had been a slave when he was young.

Now his father owned 100 acres of farmland. Benjamin was busy with all the usual farm chores. He helped his father plant and harvest crops, milk the cows, and hang the tobacco leaves in the shed to dry.

"I don't mind the farm work," he said to his sister Minta. "But I'm much happier when I'm studying. I like learning about anything and everything. Reading opens new doors for me."

Minta made a face because she did not like to study. She was also puzzled. She couldn't understand why Benjamin was always asking his grandmother for more lessons. His grandmother taught Benjamin to read and write using the only book she owned — the Bible.

"The boy has a good mind," his grandmother

told Benjamin's parents one day. "I know he'd do well in school."

Benjamin's parents looked at each other. They knew that a group of Quakers had started a school not far from the Banneker's farm. The Quakers allowed both white and black children to attend. In fact, they encouraged them.

"Well, I suppose we could let him try it," said his mother at last.

"I suppose so … as long as it doesn't get in the way of his chores," his father said. "I need him on the farm."

When Benjamin heard the news, he jumped up and down with excitement.

"You really mean it?" he cried. "I can really go to school?"

Benjamin was like a sponge in class, soaking up all the information that the teacher had to offer. He especially enjoyed the arithmetic lessons.

"Do you think we could study more complex problems?" he asked his teacher one day. "A book I read one time mentioned geometry. Could you teach us about that?"

"I'm sorry," the teacher said. "I don't know enough about higher level math. Besides, you won't need geometry to run a farm."

Benjamin didn't say anything, but he was disappointed.

"Geometry *is* important," he told himself, "and I'm going to learn about it."

When school ended that day, Benjamin walked to the home of his neighbor, Jacob Stern. Mr. Stern owned many books.

Benjamin knocked on the front door. "May I borrow a book … a geometry book?" he bravely asked Mr. Stern.

"Well, yes, I guess so," said Mr. Stern in surprise. He wondered why Benjamin would want to borrow such a text. Geometry—of all books! "I'm not sure how much you'll be able to understand. But you are welcome to use it."

During the next few weeks, Benjamin spent all of his spare time studying the fascinating new book. At night, he read it by candlelight. By day, he carried it out into the fields, sneaking a look at it as he hoed between the rows of tobacco plants.

He even kept it open on a stool beside him as he milked the cows. By the time he returned it to Mr. Stern, he had memorized every page. He had taught himself geometry.

Benjamin did not stop. He taught himself other subjects as well. He traveled around the countryside visiting his neighbors. Whenever one of them had a book about a new subject, Benjamin borrowed it. Then he studied the book day and night. Each time he returned a book, he had memorized the entire contents. Benjamin was happy with the system he had invented. By attending school and studying on his own, he was becoming quite well educated!

THEN one sad day, everything changed. Benjamin's father took him aside for a talk.

"Benjamin," he said, "I'm sorry I have to say this. But you can't go to school anymore."

"Why?" Benjamin cried in shock.

"Benjamin, I'm getting old. The work is getting too difficult for me. I can't keep up the farm by myself anymore."

"But I always do my chores," protested Benjamin.

"Yes, but I need you to help me full-time. I can't keep working all day long, every day. You're my only son. You're the only one I can turn to for help."

Benjamin stared at the ground. He could not refuse to help his father. But his heart ached when he thought of giving up his studies.

What could he do? Benjamin stayed on the farm, taking over more and more of the daily work. When his father died in 1759, Benjamin ran the farm completely. But doing nothing but planting and harvesting made him more and more depressed.

"If I don't find some way to use my mind, I'll lose it," he thought. "I have to do the farm work, and that keeps me busy twelve hours a day. But there are twelve other hours in a day. I'm going to use some of that time to do the things I love."

Benjamin set up a new schedule. He got up with the sun and worked all day on the farm. Then in the evening, when most people were climbing into bed, Benjamin began what he really wanted to do—reading and learning about new ideas. By the light of a candle at the kitchen table, he worked on mathematical puzzles, wrote poems, and created charts of the local wildlife. He was always busy. This new schedule cut into his sleep, of course. But learning about the world and how it works made him much happier than he had been before.

ONE day Benjamin was trading with a local merchant. The man knew of Benjamin's interest in anything new or different. "Let me show you something," the merchant said, taking a watch out of his coat pocket.

Benjamin was fascinated. He had heard of clocks and watches, but never before had he seen one. The regular ticking intrigued him.

"How does it work?" Benjamin asked, full of curiosity.

"I'm not sure," the merchant replied. "I just had it sent from London. If you want, you can take it home to study for a few weeks. Just bring it by the next time you're in town."

Benjamin thanked his friend and hurried home. Carefully he pried the back off the watch. As he observed the tiny gears moving smoothly together, he decided to make detailed drawings of the watch so he could build a clock of his own.

Night after night, Benjamin worked on the project. He carved each gear out of wood, since that was the only material available to him. Each evening, he whittled for hours to make each piece exactly the right size and shape. Even a tiny mistake would throw the clock out of balance and it would not run accurately.

At last, after many months, he was finished. Not sure that his wooden clock would actually work, he drew a deep breath and started it. To his amazement, it ran perfectly. Though Benjamin thought the clock experiment was an interesting challenge, he didn't realize he had done something extraordinary. In fact, his clock was the very first clock completely built in America by an American. It kept accurate time for 45 years.

NEXT Benjamin's interest turned to the stars in the sky. At night, he would lie out under the stars, observing and studying them. The damp ground soaked his clothes, and the cold wind blew into his ears until they ached. Despite the pain, the cold, and the damp, he never skipped a night. He didn't want to miss any small change in the movement of the stars.

"There must be a pattern to what is happening in the sky," he mused to himself. Benjamin had received no training in astronomy. No one taught him about the stars, yet he was able to draw charts that predicted future eclipses.

His desire to learn kept growing within him. He felt that one thing prevented him from studying and learning more.

"Farm chores keep me too busy. Cows always have to be milked in the morning and again in the evening. Crops have to be planted and then harvested. A farm takes time, and I simply don't have time for it," he explained to Minta one day.

He had dropped by her house to visit her and her husband.

It was 1783 and Benjamin was fifty-two years old. "The farm is keeping me from doing the things I want to do. So I've decided to sell it."

"What?" Minta said, staring at him in disbelief. "The farm that has belonged to our family and that we worked so hard to build?"

"Yes," said Benjamin quietly. "I've talked about it to George Ellicott. He's going to pay me twelve dollars per year. And he will let me live in the cabin. It wasn't an easy decision to make. But I think it's the right decision for me."

AT long last, Benjamin had all the free time that he wanted. He was very happy. He plunged into a new project, the art of surveying. This skill uses mathematics to measure the size, shape, and boundaries of a piece of land. Benjamin enjoyed learning the art of surveying and soon became very skillful.

In 1791, the United States government was planning to build the new capital city of Washington, D.C. Government officials needed skilled surveyors, and Thomas Jefferson, the secretary of state, suggested Benjamin Banneker. For five months, Benjamin worked in Washington, helping to shape our nation's capital.

When his work in Washington had ended, Benjamin returned to his little cabin. A new project soon challenged him. A friend encouraged him to publish an almanac. "Benjamin," said his friend, "think how important it would be for farmers to have a book that reports what kind of weather to expect."

Benjamin accepted this challenge and published an almanac each year for ten years. He made weather predictions applying what he had learned in his studies of astronomy and his observations of nature. The almanac became a very important work.

Benjamin was now probably the most famous black man in the country. He had excelled in many fields. He was an accomplished astronomer, mathematician, writer, scientist, and surveyor. He had the initiative to set his own goals and the courage to pursue his dreams.

FREDERIC TUDOR
THE ICE KING

A good businessman can see a profit where no one else has even looked. And who would ever look at a frozen pond and think of a way to make money?

Well, I did. I'm Frederic Tudor. And I have a great idea: take ice from a place where it is worthless to a place where it will bring a high price. It won't be an easy task. Many problems will have to be overcome. But I'll stick with it. I'm going to be rich!

T HERE he goes!" whispered one man.

"A madman!" exclaimed another.

"Imagine," laughed one woman. "He really expects to make money selling ice in the tropics! He's going to cut the ice here in Boston and ship it halfway around the world. It can't be done!"

Frederic Tudor knew people were making fun of him. But he was a determined man. He held his head high and kept walking through the deep snow that had fallen that January of 1806.

"Let them laugh now," he thought to himself. "Someday I will be the one laughing."

Later that day, 22-year-old Tudor went to check on the progress at the pond. Here in Boston, every pond was a source of ice each winter. When he arrived, he saw his crew hard at work.

"How much ice have you cut so far?" he asked the leader of the work crew.

"We've got about 100 tons," the crew chief replied.

"Great!" said Tudor. "You know that we are making history. By next month, we will reach our goal. We will have 130 tons of ice ready to ship to Martinique. Imagine bringing ice to that warm and lovely place! The islanders will love it! For the first time, they will see ice, touch ice, and even drink a glass of ice-cold water. And, they'll be able to keep

food in storage for longer than a day. Ice will surely change their lives."

As he spoke to the men, Frederic Tudor began to think about his past. He had been a businessman since he was thirteen. He had imported spices, teas, and other tropical products. He understood shipping expenses. Now a new idea obsessed him. Never before had anyone realized how badly ice was needed in the tropics. The technology for storing ice was in place. Surely the market for ice would flourish in the tropics! Tudor was sure he could sell Boston ice at a great profit.

THE first shipment of ice was loaded onto the ship on schedule. The journey to Martinique went smoothly.

Martinique was an island paradise. The clear blue water shimmered under the rays of the sun. Tall palm trees lined the beautiful sandy beach. The islanders welcomed Tudor's ship and extended their hospitality to his men. But once the ice was unloaded, things began to go wrong. To Tudor's amazement, the people of Martinique had no interest in ice. The idea of cold drinks made them suspicious. Ice was strange and frightening. Never before had they experienced anything that cold.

"Go ahead. Touch it," Tudor encouraged one man, holding out a piece of ice to him.

Fearfully the man extended his arm. When his finger hit the cold, wet ice, he screamed and ran away.

"What's wrong?" Tudor asked a crew member who understood French and could talk to the people.

"He thinks his finger is burned," the crewman said, shaking his head. "He just doesn't understand ice."

What could Tudor do with a shipload of ice no one wanted? He searched for an answer. That afternoon he met a man who ran a local restaurant. Tudor showed him how to use ice to make ice cream. He taught him how to make cold drinks and serve chilled fruits. After the man tasted the ice cream and the chilled fruit, he decided to buy forty pounds of ice. That night he made $300 selling ice cream to amazed customers.

As the people of Martinique developed a taste for ice cream, cold drinks, and chilled foods, a demand for ice was created. Ice became popular. But by then, Tudor had another problem that needed his attention. The ice was melting.

"What I need is a better way to store my blocks of ice," he thought. "They need more protection. This hot weather is unlike anything we have in Boston!"

But the ice just kept on melting. Six weeks after arriving in Martinique, Tudor's ice had turned to water. He had not made any money on the trip. In fact, he had lost about $4,000. He was discouraged.

WHEN he returned to Boston, Tudor admitted that he had made some mistakes. But he knew the idea could be successful. One failure would not change his mind.

For the next several years, Tudor continued to pour money into the ice business. He concentrated on designing a good icehouse. He needed one that could store ice for months, not just days or weeks. At first he worked underground. He could keep almost half the ice solid through a hot summer season. But more than half melted.

Each year, his fellow Bostonians laughed louder and louder. They were astonished at Frederic Tudor's perseverance and determination.

"The only thing more foolish than sending ice to Martinique," they joked, "is sending ice to Martinique twice."

Tudor was indifferent to their mockery. He created new designs and worked to improve his methods. To test his new designs, he traveled to Cuba where he knew he would have to protect the ice from the warm, tropical climate. There, he tried many different ways to keep ice from melting.

First, he wrapped it in blankets. Then, he packed it in straw. He even sprinkled wood chips on it.

Suddenly, things began to work for him! He was able to keep more than 90 percent of the ice from melting.

"It's not perfect," he thought, "but I hope it's good enough."

To his dismay, a new problem arose. Starting in 1818, Boston experienced several mild winters. The ice on many New England ponds never became thick enough to cut. Tudor knew what to do. He would send his crew to northern Canada.

"What do we do up there?" a crew member asked Tudor.

"We need ice. If we can't find it in Boston, we'll find it in Canada. We'll chop ice off icebergs," Tudor told him humorously.

But, secretly, Tudor was worried. This task was very difficult, and it proved very expensive as well. He had to make a profit soon or he would have to give up.

LUCKILY, Tudor met Nathaniel Wyeth, an inventor who loved a challenge. He offered to become Tudor's assistant.

Wyeth began to help Tudor with a series of inventions. One invention was an ice cutter drawn by horses. With this new machine, blocks of ice could be cut faster and easier than by hand. Another invention was an ice scraper. This machine allowed men to scrape snow off the ice before cutting it. These inventions made harvesting ice cheaper and easier. Tudor was delighted. But Wyeth saved his best idea for last.

"I can cut the melting rate of your packed ice," he told Tudor.

"It's already down to eight percent," said Tudor. "How much more can you cut it?"

"I can cut the melting rate to zero," Wyeth replied.

"How?" gasped Tudor.

"The secret is sawdust," said Wyeth. "Experiment. Pack your ice in sawdust and see what happens."

That winter, Tudor took a few blocks of ice and followed Wyeth's advice. To his joy, the ice stayed solid through the entire summer. In spite of hot days and nights, the ice did not melt at all.

"Now I can ship ice anywhere in the world!" Tudor cried excitedly. He hurried to his office and began working on a grand new plan.

"Next year," he announced to his crew, "we are going to travel to Calcutta, India!"

"But that's halfway around the world," one man protested.

"We'll have to cross the Equator twice to get there," added another.

"Don't worry," Tudor insisted. "The ice won't melt, and the trip will be a great success. It will be very profitable for us."

The crew members had their doubts. And once again, the people of Boston laughed at Tudor's plan.

"It'll never work," people said. "Sawdust can't keep ice frozen all the way to India!"

IN May of 1833, the ship with its cargo of ice set off on the four-month journey to India. When it finally arrived, not a single block of ice had melted.

Since India was a British colony, many people from Great Britain were living there. They, of course, were very familiar with ice and its uses. They welcomed Tudor's ice with great enthusiasm. The ice sold quickly, and Tudor made a handsome profit.

Ice was a new experience for the native Indians, however. They had much to learn about this unknown material. Many of them wanted their money back after their purchases melted in the sun. Some put their ice in water to keep it; others put salt on it. The salt made it disappear even faster! They thought it must be magical.

Ice was magical, in a way, for Tudor. He had proved that he could take ice to the tropics. He kept trying his idea until it was a success. The people of Boston looked at him with new respect. His growing ice business had helped Boston become a booming port city.

The Ice King became a man of many "firsts." His mind never stopped working. He designed a new hull for ships. He brought the first steam locomotive to Boston. He even developed the first amusement park in the United States. The Ice King was really a king of ideas.

FRANCIS SCOTT KEY

"THE STAR-SPANGLED BANNER"

I never knew I would be there on that terrible night. The sky was ablaze with lights—frightening lights. Rockets crashed against the walls of the fort. And the sound echoes still—the crash and boom of the cannonballs hurtling against those massive walls.

But I *was* there ... Francis Scott Key, lawyer, public servant, American citizen. And I'll never forget waiting for the final outcome.

THE British have captured Washington, D.C.! They're burning the capital of the United States! They have taken many prisoners! Who knows what they will do next!" The word spread from town to town.

For two weeks, from August 24 to September 7, 1814, Francis Scott Key, a young lawyer, waited anxiously with other Americans. The War of 1812 had been going on for two years, but never before had it been so close and so devastating. Would the British regain control of America?

No one knew exactly where or when the British would attack.

"The British are regrouping back in Chesapeake Bay," one soldier said.

"They're planning to attack Baltimore," another said.

Every city close to Washington, D.C., was in danger and the citizens feared they would be captured by the enemy.

Wild rumors about prisoners of war began to spread. Respected citizens, it seemed, were missing. They were believed to be on the English ships, chained together down below. The thought was harrowing.

One day, news of a particular prisoner reached Francis Scott Key.

"I've just heard that Dr. William Beanes was captured. He is being held near Baltimore," an anxious Francis Key said to John S. Skinner, the American colonel in charge of prisoner exchanges. "He is a dear friend and a noble citizen. What can I do to help?"

"As a matter of fact, I'm working to free your friend," the colonel told him. "I need a brave man to assist me."

So, on September 7, Key and Colonel Skinner climbed into a small boat and raised a white flag of truce alongside the boat's American flag. They sailed toward the British fleet in Chesapeake Bay. British General Robert Ross allowed them to board the British ship *Tonnant*.

"I honor your white flag of truce," the general told them. "State your purpose."

Key and Colonel Skinner explained their mission. After much discussion and bargaining with General Ross, they struck a deal. Key and Skinner would release letters from British prisoners of war. In exchange, General Ross agreed to release Dr. Beanes.

As Key and Skinner prepared to leave, they overheard General Ross discuss plans for his upcoming attack on Baltimore.

"The attack will begin on September 13," they heard General Ross say. "We will destroy Fort McHenry, the fort that guards the city of Baltimore. Then, Baltimore will have to surrender."

Francis Scott Key's pulse began to race. So *that* was the British plan! Oh, he must somehow get word to Major Armistead at Fort McHenry! The major must gather the entire American army to fend off the attack. Baltimore must not fall!

General Ross turned sharply, suspiciously. His voice was cold as he spoke to Key and Skinner: "Gentlemen. Unfortunately, you have overheard our plans. You will have to stay here until the battle is over, and we are victorious."

"You're taking us prisoner?" cried Key.

"No, not at all. When the attack is over, you may leave. But we cannot let you go until then."

Key and the colonel looked at each other. They

felt the same frustration. If only they could get the priceless information to their fellow Americans! But they were powerless. For the next few days, they could only pace the deck helplessly.

EARLY on September 13, British ships began moving stealthily up the Patapsco River toward Fort McHenry. Francis Scott Key and Colonel John Skinner turned to their guards.

"Please," Skinner pleaded, "if we must remain here during the attack, at least let us watch the battle on a ship that flies the American flag."

The guards consulted with the general. He decided to put all the Americans on the prisoner-exchange ship behind the British fleet. He wanted them out of the way during the battle.

Back on his own ship, Key felt a little better. He knew he and his companions could not sail toward shore or the British guards would surely shoot them. But at least they could watch the battle in the company of Americans.

As the group waited nervously for the attack to begin, Key pulled out a spyglass that magnified the scene and gave him a clear view of Fort McHenry, eight miles away.

"Look at this," he cried. "Major Armistead is flying a huge American flag over the fort."

It was true. A flag that measured 30 feet by 42 feet had been raised. It was almost as wide and high as the side of a barn. The major had told his men: "I want a flag that the British can see from a distance. I want them to know that America has not surrendered."

SUDDENLY, at 7:00 A.M., the British opened fire. From two miles away, they shelled the ramparts, the high walls of Fort McHenry. All morning their guns blasted, chipping away at the walls of the fort. The smaller American guns, however, could not reach the British ships. The British were safe as they bombarded the fort.

"I'm afraid it's just a matter of time," Dr. Beanes said sadly.

"You may be right," Key admitted. "I don't

know how long Major Armistead can hold out. How much shelling can the fort endure?"

As the morning wore on, the three men on the American ship kept watch through their spyglass. They expected Fort McHenry to collapse and surrender at any moment. But as the noonday sun rose high in the sky, the American flag still fluttered proudly over Fort McHenry.

"As long as that flag is flying, we know our men are still holding on," Key declared.

Twilight came. Fort McHenry had endured a whole day of shelling. Then something changed.

"They must be going in to capture the fort," Key said grimly as he watched the British ships move in closer to the fort.

But suddenly, as the British came within range, the Americans opened fire with their cannon.

"Wait!" cried Key to the others. "The tide of battle is turning! The British are pulling back! They're retreating! The fort's cannon is damaging their ships. This fight isn't over yet!"

Through his spyglass, Key saw the British turning around to move out of range of the American cannon. Safe from American guns, they began shelling the fort again.

As darkness fell, the one-sided battle continued. Key, Skinner, and Dr. Beanes waited in fear and suspense. Again and again they saw British rockets sizzling through the air. The bursting bombs lit up the night sky with red fire and shook the men on board the small ship. With each explosion, Key felt a wave of despair. How much more shelling could Fort McHenry stand? Surely each explosion must be causing damage.

T HEN at 4:00 A.M. of the second day, the shelling stopped. Rockets no longer brightened the sky. Everything was black and silent. The sudden silence was more frightening than the bombardments.

"What does this mean?" Colonel Skinner cried out. "Has the fort fallen? Have the Americans surrendered? What has happened?"

Neither Key nor Dr. Beanes could answer him, for they had no way of knowing. They took turns with the spyglass, straining to see some hint of activity. The dark night sky revealed nothing.

"At least when the bombs were falling, they lit up the sky and we could see the flag still flying," said Key. "Now I fear the worst."

Dr. Beanes spoke, his voice shaking, "All we can do is wait. When dawn comes, we will know the outcome."

It seemed night would never end. Finally, day began to break. But a dense fog had settled in and the anxious men still could not see a thing.

Time crawled by. Then, a little after daybreak, the fog started to lift.

Key peered through the spyglass. His heart raced.

"There it is!" he shouted. "The flag! The American flag! It's still flying! And look! The British are retreating down the river!"

Choking with emotion, Key turned and embraced his companions. The three men shouted with joy. Dr. Beanes and the colonel did a little dance on the deck.

As Key watched them, words began to form in his head. His heart was full. He had seen great courage and great patriotism. He pulled an envelope from his pocket. On the back of it, he jotted down some lines of poetry. He began by speaking of his fear and hope that incredible morning: "Oh say, can you see by the dawn's early light, what so proudly we hailed at the twilight's last gleaming?" He wrote of the hours spent watching the flag survive the bombs and rockets. He ended his poem, his heart filled with love and hope: "Oh say, does that star-spangled banner yet wave o'er the land of the free and the home of the brave?"

LATER that night, Key, Skinner, and Dr. Beanes returned to Baltimore. They saw their own relief and joy reflected on the face of every citizen they passed. Before going to bed, Francis Scott Key took the envelope out of his pocket. As he studied the lines of his poem, he knew it was destined to become a song.

The next morning, Key showed his work to John Skinner.

"It doesn't have a title yet," Key said, "but I think it could be sung to a familiar tune."

Skinner loved the poem. He sent it to a publisher that very day. It was printed on handbills and distributed throughout Baltimore. After a few days, the poem was set to a popular tune. Soon everyone in Baltimore was singing and marching to Francis Scott Key's song. The men at Fort McHenry especially loved the song. Francis Scott Key had captured the drama of that September night. Within a few weeks, the entire nation was singing it.

People called Key's song "The Star-Spangled Banner." In time, it became America's national anthem. The song reminds all of us of the time when America was fighting for its survival.

CHARLES GOODYEAR
THE MYSTERY OF RUBBER

Should I believe Charles Goodyear anymore? He came to me so convinced he had made a wonderful discovery. I lent him the money to develop his product, then it turned out to be a flop. I'm a businessman. I can't afford to lose money.

But here he is again! He says he has perfected his idea, and that it will make us both millionaires. Dare I believe him?

THIS isn't right," Charles Goodyear sighed as he surveyed the mess in the middle of his cell. He sat alone in a dark Philadelphia debtor's prison. Goodyear was convinced that he could find a way of treating raw rubber to make it useful. Raw rubber turned hard and brittle on cold days, sticky and soft on hot days. If only he could find a way to make it resistant to the weather! He felt certain he could if he had enough money and time. He had the time, but not the money! He was in prison for not paying his debts.

"Rubber is a wonderful substance," he kept telling his wife, Clarissa, when she came to visit him. "It's strong, it stretches, it sheds water. Think of all the things that could be made out of it!"

"But it is always changing. It doesn't last," she

"You're always making false promises," sputtered his neighbors. "You're always exaggerating the truth."

"I'm through with you," said the friend who had loaned him the money. "You and your ridiculous experiments! I risked my money on your idea, and you've failed."

Again, Goodyear apologized for his mistake. But he still had faith in his idea. He couldn't find any more wealthy supporters in Philadelphia. No one wanted to take a chance on a man who had failed twice. So with a small loan from relatives, he moved his wife and four children to a home in New Haven, Connecticut. Here he hoped to find new support for his idea. New Haven, however, contained few friendly faces. People showed no enthusiasm for Goodyear's ideas. No one would lend him money.

"I can see I will have to do this alone," Goodyear said to Clarissa gloomily.

He set to work. He turned the Goodyear kitchen into a laboratory for rubber experiments. He worked longer and longer hours. Every morning he got up before sunrise and worked without stopping until late afternoon.

ONE day he was still working when Clarissa came to make supper. She lit the stove and put some water on to boil. "I'm sorry to interrupt you, but the children are hungry, and I must prepare supper."

Goodyear did not answer. He was too absorbed in his latest effort. This time he was mixing the rubber with sulphur. As he stirred the mixture, some of it splashed out onto the hot stove. Goodyear was annoyed with himself for making such a mess.

He started to clean it up, then he stopped and stared. The glob of spilled rubber did not melt as it always had before. Instead, it became solid like leather, yet flexible. The heat had changed the mixture in some way. The rubber lost its stickiness and gained new strength. Goodyear knew then that he had stumbled onto something wonderful. He had found the secret!

"Clarissa!" he shouted. "Clarissa, look at this!

I've found it! I've found the way to keep rubber from melting."

Clarissa peered over his shoulder.

"Yes, I see," she said doubtfully, "but what will happen when it gets cold? Will it crack and break?"

"Let's find out!" Goodyear said. He poured more of the mixture into a pan and heated it, creating a large sheet of rubber. Then he took the sheet outside. After breaking icicles off the side of the house, he nailed the sheet to the wall.

The next morning Goodyear rushed to look at the sheet of rubber. To his delight, it had not hardened. It was exactly the way he had hung it—soft and flexible.

"Hurray! I've done it!" he shouted across the snowy field. "I've solved the mystery of rubber!"

UNFORTUNATELY, Goodyear's troubles were not over. This time he truly had created a wonderful new type of rubber. But nobody believed him.

"Please," he begged local businessmen. "Please loan me some money so that I can perfect my discovery."

But these businessmen simply turned their backs and walked away. Even family members refused to help Goodyear. No one wanted to hear about his newest discovery. For the next five years, Goodyear traveled around New England. Everywhere he went, he begged for money to perfect and produce his new form of rubber. He wanted to make new rubber products. But everyone turned him down.

At long last, in 1844, Goodyear convinced his brother-in-law to provide him with enough money to continue his testing and perfect his formula. On June 15, the government granted him a patent. The patent gave him, and him alone, the right to use his process for producing rubber. The process he developed allowed rubber to remain flexible yet strong in cold and hot weather. This process was called "vulcanization," after Vulcan, the Roman god of fire.

Now rubber could be used for many different products, for life preservers, rubber bands, raincoats, hoses, and watertight seals. People finally began to take notice of his discovery.

Goodyear never did become rich. But he helped create an important new industry in America and lived to see it flourish. He took comfort in knowing that he had been right all along. There was a way to unlock the secret of rubber. After years of trying, he, Charles Goodyear, had found it.

SAMUEL F. B. MORSE

INVENTOR OF THE TELEGRAPH

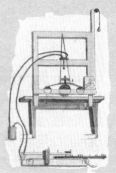

Gentlemen, think back on the War of 1812. The bloodiest battle of that war was fought needlessly. Peace had already been declared. Yet, tragically, 2,000 of our finest young men were sent to their deaths. Why? Because we didn't know about the peace treaty. News had not reached America yet.

Such a tragedy need never happen again. I stand before you today with a system that will provide instant communication.

I'M so tired of painting portraits!" Samuel F. B. Morse sighed to himself as he packed up his easel and left his client's house. "I can't even afford to have a studio and let customers come to me. I have to travel from town to town, just so I can make enough money to get by."

Morse bought a newspaper and checked into a hotel for the night. Exhausted, he sank into a chair and looked for something cheerful to read. An article about the rebuilding of the Capitol Building in Washington caught his eye: "Upon completion of the building, the nation's finest artists will be commissioned to decorate the inside walls with murals."

Morse's heart thumped wildly. He had always dreamed of painting great, majestic historical murals. He resolved to be one of the artists chosen to decorate the Capitol Building.

"I must return to Europe and train myself to paint the best murals the world has ever seen!"

Morse studied three years in Europe. He sought out the best teachers and viewed the world's art masterpieces for techniques and inspiration. But his money ran out, and in 1832 he had to return to America.

On the voyage across the Atlantic Ocean, he chanced to be seated at the same dinner table one evening with a man named Dr. Charles Jackson. This gentleman had just acquired an interesting new device, an electromagnet, and was so excited about it that he discussed it with everyone.

"It's so simple," he exclaimed. "An electromagnet is just a piece of iron curved like a horseshoe with wire wrapped around it. Whenever an electric current passes through the wire, the iron becomes a magnet."

A passenger asked, "How long does it take the electricity to pass through the wire?"

"Instantly!" Dr. Jackson replied. "Electricity can travel even long distances instantly!"

Morse knew about electricity from his college days. He began to think about the possibility of using it to transmit information over many miles. What an idea! He spent the rest of the voyage sketching such a system. He called it an electric "telegraph" from the Greek words "far writer."

Morse's telegraph included three elements: a sending unit, a receiving unit, and a special code. The sending unit was a device that would send out bursts of electricity. Each burst would travel through the wire until it reached a magnet on the other end. The bursts would cause the magnet to drop onto a piece of paper, leaving a mark. Using a special code of dots, dashes, and spaces that Morse developed, the marks could be translated into letters and numbers.

BACK in the United States, Morse became consumed by two passions: painting and his telegraph. He had to rely on painting to support him. He became a professor of art at the University of the City of New York. He wasn't paid a salary, and he had to give private lessons to earn money.

He kept working on his model of the telegraph in his spare time. The telegraph didn't cost much — he made it out of scraps of materials that he found. By 1836, he had completed a model.

His hopes were high, too, for a chance to paint the murals in the new Capitol Building. The time had come for Congress to choose the mural painters, and Morse tensely awaited the decision. Surely Congress would recognize his undeniable talent and award him the $10,000! His financial problems would be over. He would paint historical murals that the entire nation would view with awe.

At last, the announcement came. Morse had not been chosen. Tears filled his eyes. All his plans meant nothing now. He felt destroyed.

"I shall never paint again!" he exclaimed. "My hopes and dreams have ended only in disappointment. I grieve for this lost opportunity. Never again will I put brush to paper!"

So turning totally away from painting, Morse devoted himself entirely to work on his telegraph model.

"You've got to believe me," he told his friend Alfred Vail in September 1837. "This is really a great idea. I just need some money so I can go to Washington and apply for a patent for this telegraph. The world grows larger every day, and it's important to be able to send messages quickly. With my machine, no one will have to depend upon horses or trains."

Vail and his father, Stephen, agreed to help Morse. They owned the Speedwell Iron Works in New Jersey and recognized the importance of fast communication in the business world. The financial market in New York City would be able to communicate with the cotton market in New Orleans, for example, within a matter of minutes instead of weeks.

STEPHEN Vail loaned Morse money, and Alfred helped him complete the model. In 1838, Morse left for Washington, D.C. He made a passionate speech to Congress and gave them a demonstration of his model.

"This is the machine of the future," he told them. "Think of it: instant communication from house to house, town to town, city to city."

The members of Congress seemed interested. A congressman from Maine was especially excited. He was Francis Ormond Jonathan Smith—"Fog" for short—and he proposed that Congress give Morse the money for the telegraph.

"Give him $30,000 and let him build a telegraph from Baltimore to Washington, D.C.," Fog said.

"But that's over forty miles," said one senator.

"That's the whole point!" said Fog. "Let's see how well the thing works over long distances."

The members of Congress discussed it. Some supported Fog's suggestion. But others didn't think the government should spend money on such an untried idea. In the end, Congress voted against awarding money to Morse.

"I can't do anything without federal funding," Morse said, shaking his head sadly .

"Don't give up," Fog encouraged. "Try again. Be persistent. Congress is sure to give you the money sooner or later."

Morse shrugged. "Maybe," he muttered.

For the next five years, Morse drifted. He kept working on his telegraph and trying to build up interest in it. He patented his machine in the United States, but his attempts to patent it in England and France failed. The next session of Congress did not fund his project, either.

FINALLY, in 1843, he summoned his courage and returned to Washington once again to ask for funding. While Congress debated the proposal, Morse paced the floors of his boarding house waiting for news from Fog Smith. Finally, on the last day of the session, Fog rushed into Morse's room.

"Guess what?" he roared. "They passed it! You've got your $30,000!"

"Is it true?" shouted Morse, jumping to his feet.

"It is!" cried Fog. "And guess what else? *My* construction company is going to lay all 41 miles of wire."

"Great!" Morse exclaimed joyously. Finally, his dream had come true.

For days Morse hurried here and there making arrangements. He was eager to complete the laying of wire. But his joy turned sour. Fog Smith's construction crew was a disaster. The crew members had no sense of urgency. They worked slowly and spent money very quickly. Before long, they had spent $23,000. And only a few miles of wire were laid. At this rate, there would not be enough money to complete the project.

"This is ridiculous!" Morse fumed. He decided to get rid of Fog and his crew, and in February 1844, hired a man named Ezra Cornell. Cornell's

men worked quickly and efficiently. Morse hoped that now things would run smoothly.

The second day on the job, however, Cornell came to Morse with bad news.

"We have to replace the wire Fog's crew laid down. Fog used wire wrapped in cotton. The cotton burned off when the wire got hot, and now the wire won't carry electricity at all."

Morse was in a frenzy. "All my hopes depend on this one project. If it falls through, I'll be ruined. I'll be a complete failure," he moaned. He decided to change technique. Instead of laying wire underground, he chose to string it on tall chestnut poles. Broken bottle necks on top of the poles served as insulators.

AT last, in May 1844, Cornell's crew finished putting up the wire. Now came the big moment. On May 24, Samuel Finley Breese Morse stood before his telegraph in the Capitol Building in Washington, D.C. At the other end of the line, in Baltimore, Alfred Vail and an eager audience waited. As all held their breath, Morse tapped out his now famous message: "What hath God wrought!"

Samuel F. B. Morse had succeeded. He had created the first telegraph system in the world. Now messages could be sent from city to city in a matter of minutes. Business deals that had taken two to four weeks through the mail could now be completed in one day. Merchants could order shipments directly from factories. Railroads could make schedule and track changes to prevent accidents. Newspapers could report the latest events from all over the country. A family in Washington that had heard rumors of a death of a relative in New York could find out immediately if it were true.

Before long, telegraph lines stretched across the entire United States. In 1858, a telegraph cable was completed under the Atlantic Ocean, connecting Europe and America. Messages tapped out in Morse code united the two continents. By 1900, almost every town in the nation had a telegraph office. Morse had used his talents well. He had given the world instant communication.

ELIZABETH BLACKWELL

AMERICA'S FIRST WOMAN DOCTOR

A warm April breeze blew gently through the tenement window. As a woman washed dishes, a child's scream filled the air. The young mother flew out the door. Her five-year-old's hand was badly cut. What could she do? Who could she turn to for help? How she wished there was an understanding doctor in her neighborhood.

ELIZABETH Blackwell coughed nervously as she entered the bedroom of her sick friend. Matilda Ross lay on the bed, thin, pale, and weak. Elizabeth cringed when she saw her. At the same age, 23, Elizabeth was in perfect health. She had no experience with pain and suffering. She wasn't sure what to say to ailing Matilda.

"Matilda," she whispered softly. "How are you feeling?"

"It's very bad," came Matilda's faint answer.

"Have the doctors found out what is wrong with you?"

"Oh, Elizabeth, they haven't helped at all! They don't listen to me. They don't even talk to me — it's terrible. Maybe if the doctors were women, they would understand better. As it is … I feel completely alone."

Matilda looked up at Elizabeth with sunken eyes. "What I need," she said weakly, "is someone like you — someone kind and helpful and understanding. You should go into medicine, Elizabeth — you'd be a wonderful doctor."

"Me?" Elizabeth exclaimed. "I don't know the first thing about medicine! Besides, there are no women doctors. You know that. There never have been and there probably never will be."

"Too bad," Matilda said weakly. "Such a shame ... "

A few weeks later, in the spring of 1844, Matilda died.

Elizabeth cried for hours when she heard the news. She couldn't believe that her beautiful young friend had died. As she lay grieving, Matilda's words ran through her head. *You should go into medicine, Elizabeth — you'd be a wonderful doctor.*

Two days later, Elizabeth sat down with her eight brothers and sisters in their home in Cincinnati, Ohio.

"I have an announcement to make," she said calmly. "I have decided to become a doctor."

"Really?" asked her sister Emily in disbelief.

"Can girls do that?" asked little Anna.

"Why don't you just become a nurse like other women?" asked her brother Samuel.

Elizabeth had hoped for more support. But she stuck to her decision.

"I want to be a doctor," she declared firmly. "And somehow, someday, I *will* be one."

That September, Elizabeth Blackwell took a job as a schoolteacher to earn money. At night she began to prepare herself for a career in medicine. A kindly old doctor helped her with her studies.

After three years of studying, Blackwell felt ready for medical school. She applied to every medical college in the country.

"Now," she murmured to herself, "there's nothing I can do but wait."

She didn't have long to wait. Letters started flying back from the schools. The letters expressed shock that a woman would dare to apply to medical school. The schools would not even consider her application.

"Young women would do better if they prepared to be nurses," one school replied.

"Our male students would refuse to sit in class with a female," wrote another.

As each rejection letter arrived, Blackwell became more and more depressed. Finally, she had only one chance left. She had not heard from the Geneva Medical College in western New York. When this medical college finally sent her a reply, Blackwell opened it anxiously. To her surprise, it was not a letter of rejection.

"They've accepted me!" she shouted joyfully, dancing around the room.

IN the fall of 1847, Blackwell moved to the little college town of Geneva. On the first day of classes, she gathered her books and walked to the lecture hall. The male students immediately began whistling and jeering. Blackwell felt her cheeks flush red with embarrassment. But she kept walking. She took her seat. She looked straight ahead and ignored the taunts.

"I must not show any weakness," she thought frantically as she opened her notebook. "On the outside, at least, I must remain calm and poised."

When class ended, Blackwell stood up. The teasing started again. Blackwell felt like crying, but she held her head high as she walked out of the classroom. Male students followed her all the way across campus. They laughed and whistled and shouted rude remarks.

"You think you were accepted to this college on your merit?" they jeered. "You were accepted as a practical joke!"

They followed her to her rooming house.

"You're never going to be a doctor! You should go back home where you belong!"

When Blackwell reached her room, she collapsed on the bed and buried her head in her pillow.

"Is it going to be like this all year?" she wondered in despair. "Will these men ridicule me forever?"

After a while, Blackwell forced herself to get up. "There is no sense in feeling sorry for myself," she told herself sternly. "If I am going to make it as a doctor, I've got to be strong. And starting right now, I'm going to study harder than anyone. I'll show them I'm no joke!"

For the next few weeks, Blackwell endured the constant ribbing and teasing of her classmates. During that time, she proved just how strong she was. She never broke down because of the teasing. The ribbing never made her angry or upset. No matter how the male students tried to rile her, she ignored them and kept studying.

One day during a lecture on anatomy, a student threw a note at Blackwell. It landed on her arm as she sat writing in her notebook. She felt nervous. She knew the note probably contained an insulting comment. She also knew that every student in the room was waiting, watching to see what she would do.

"This is it," she told herself. "If I lose my self-control, the battle will be lost."

So she let the note sit on her arm, unopened, while she continued taking notes. When class ended, she slowly raised her arm into the air. Then she flicked her wrist as if ridding herself of an annoying insect. The note fell to the floor.

With that gesture, she won the hearts of her fellow students. At last they understood. They realized that she was serious about studying medicine, and that nothing was going to stop her. Impressed with her style, the students broke into applause. From that day on, no one ever bothered Blackwell again. She became just another member of the class.

IN January 1849, Blackwell completed her studies at Geneva Medical College and received her degree.

"I did it!" she wrote with pride to her sister Emily. "I'm now a doctor!"

But for Blackwell, this was only the beginning.

"I want to be a surgeon," she continued, "so I need extra training. And the best place to get it is in Europe."

By June, Blackwell was a resident doctor in a Paris hospital. At first her work went well. But one day she treated a baby with an infected eye. As she worked on the child, her own eye started to itch. Without thinking, she reached up and

rubbed it. When she did that, she transmitted the child's infection into her own eye.

Soon Blackwell's eyes became swollen and red. She developed a high fever as the infection spread through her body. For days she lay helplessly in bed. At times, she seemed near death. Finally, the fever subsided and Blackwell began to get well. The infection had done terrible damage, however. It left her blind in one eye, and it weakened the other eye. Without good eyesight, she knew she could never become a surgeon.

Once again, Blackwell refused to pity herself.

"Well," she told herself, "I can't be a surgeon, but I am a doctor. I can still help people who are suffering."

IN 1850, Blackwell returned to New York City to open her own practice. However, new trials lay ahead. No landlord wanted to rent office space to a woman doctor.

"Please," she begged one man who owned several buildings. "Please just let me rent one small office. I promise that you won't regret it."

"All right," the man said reluctantly, "but no advertising. I don't even want to see a sign on the door with your name on it. If my other renters found out I was renting to a woman doctor, they would all move out. So *no* signs. Understand?"

"Yes," Blackwell sighed, "I understand."

Since she couldn't advertise, Blackwell had no way to let people know that she was a doctor. She had very few patients. After many slow months, she knew something had to change.

"I'm not doing any good here," she thought to herself. "There are people out there who need me. I've just got to find them."

THEN Blackwell had an idea. "I know!" she cried. "I'll open a clinic in the poorest neighborhood in town. The people there can use my help."

Boldly she rented a small, shabby room in a rundown section of the city. She announced that it was a clinic for women and children. At first she stood outside on the sidewalk, chatting with the women who walked by. She gave out free advice, free examinations, and free medicine.

"Pay me if you can," she told her grateful patients. "If you can't, then forget about it."

Soon Blackwell had plenty of business at her one-woman clinic. Poor women from all over the city came to see her. They came with questions about health, hygiene, child care, and nutrition. Blackwell told them everything they wanted to know. They adored her, and she in turn loved and cared for them.

Blackwell's clinic was so successful that in 1857 she decided to expand it. She spent months raising money and fixing up an old building. Two younger women worked with her. One of them was her sister Emily, who had followed her example and become a doctor and a surgeon. The other was a young woman recently graduated from medical school. Blackwell had helped and encouraged her to study medicine earlier.

With her partners standing next to her, Blackwell flung open the doors of the new hospital for women. It was the first hospital ever to boast an all-female staff.

As Blackwell looked at the patients filing in the door, she felt a lump rise in her throat.

"I always knew I could do it," she thought. She remembered her friend who had died so many years before. "Matilda would be proud of me."

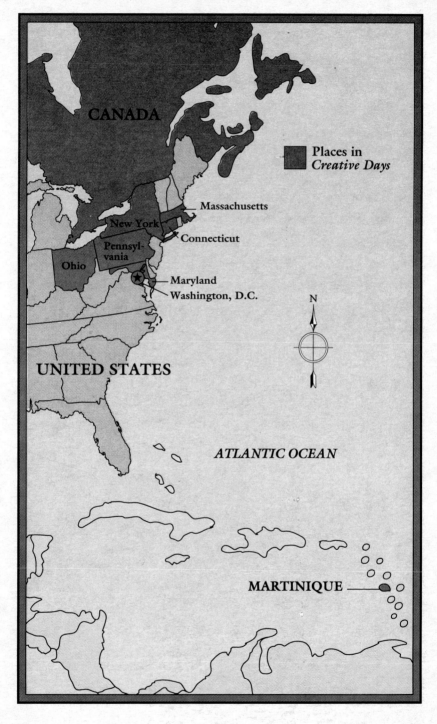

Places in
Creative Days

CANADA

Massachusetts

New York

Connecticut

Pennsyl-
vania

Ohio

Maryland

Washington, D.C.

N

UNITED STATES

ATLANTIC OCEAN

MARTINIQUE